ALL ABOUT SHARKS
SHARK ATTACKS

By Gail Terp

BrightPoint Press

San Diego, CA

© 2023 BrightPoint Press
an imprint of ReferencePoint Press, Inc.
Printed in the United States

For more information, contact:
BrightPoint Press
PO Box 27779
San Diego, CA 92198
www.BrightPointPress.com

ALL RIGHTS RESERVED.

No part of this work covered by the copyright hereon may be reproduced or used in any form or by any means—graphic, electronic, or mechanical, including photocopying, recording, taping, web distribution, or information storage retrieval systems—without the written permission of the publisher.

LIBRARY OF CONGRESS CATALOGING-IN-PUBLICATION DATA

Names: Terp, Gail, 1951- author.
Title: Shark attacks / by Gail Terp.
Description: San Diego, CA: BrightPoint Press, [2023] | Series: All about sharks | Includes bibliographical references and index. | Audience: Grades 10-12
Identifiers: LCCN 2022008570 (print) | LCCN 2022008571 (eBook) | ISBN 9781678203689 (hardcover) | ISBN 9781678203696 (eBook)
Subjects: LCSH: Shark attacks--Juvenile literature.
Classification: LCC QL638.93 .T47 2023 (print) | LCC QL638.93 (eBook) | DDC 597.3/3--dc23/eng/20220314
LC record available at https://lccn.loc.gov/2022008570
LC eBook record available at https://lccn.loc.gov/2022008571

CONTENTS

AT A GLANCE	4
INTRODUCTION	6
WHY STUDY SHARK ATTACKS?	
CHAPTER ONE	12
HOW BIG A RISK?	
CHAPTER TWO	26
THE MOST DANGEROUS SHARKS	
CHAPTER THREE	38
LIVED TO TELL	
CHAPTER FOUR	48
STAYING SAFE IN THE WATER	
Glossary	58
Source Notes	59
For Further Research	60
Index	62
Image Credits	63
About the Author	64

AT A GLANCE

- A shark can detect the tiny bits of electricity that prey makes when it moves.

- Sharks have three ways to attack their prey. These are hit-and-run, bump-and-bite, and sneak attacks.

- There is no proof that sharks actively hunt humans. However, some human actions can lead to a higher risk of attack.

- There are hundreds of kinds of sharks, but only about twelve are a danger to humans.

- The United States and Australia have the most shark attacks each year.

- Scientists have discovered a 3,000-year-old human skeleton with shark bite marks.

- Shark experts say that people shouldn't go in the water at dawn or dusk. This is a top feeding time for sharks.

- To keep from attracting sharks, people should not wear shiny jewelry or bright swimsuits.

INTRODUCTION

WHY STUDY SHARK ATTACKS?

March 18, 2021, was not the fun day Bryce Albert expected. As the 20-year-old was standing in chest-high water on a Florida beach, all was well. Then he felt a hard bump on his arm. Curious, he raised his arm out of the water. It was bleeding badly. Something had bitten him.

Albert didn't know what. He didn't panic, but he did get to shore as fast as he could. He shielded his injured arm to avoid

Some beaches have signs warning visitors of possible sharks.

Blacktip sharks are found in warm waters around the world. This causes them to encounter people often.

scaring anyone. Once on the beach, a lifeguard bandaged Albert's arm and a friend drove him to the hospital.

Albert was in the hospital for six days. He had two successful surgeries. The doctors studied his wound. They said it was likely caused by a blacktip shark about six feet (1.8 m) in length. In spite of the attack, Albert thought he would return to the water after his wound healed. He said, "The odds of this happening, it was like 1 in 3.75 million. I grew up in the water, I love it. I don't want to be scared of it, so I think I'm going to at least try my best not to be."[1]

RESEARCH LEADS THE WAY

Shark attacks are scary events. To lessen fear, researchers study sharks. They find out which shark **species** are most likely to attack. They identify when and where attacks most often occur. Their research shows what ocean conditions are most likely to cause the attacks. It highlights what human actions tend to lead to them.

Research informs people of the safest times of day to enter the water. They learn what areas to avoid. They also learn what attracts sharks. This information can reduce fear of sharks and promote safety.

Scientists often dive to study sharks. Cages help keep them safe.

1

HOW BIG A RISK?

The first known shark attack report was written in 1580. While sailing from Portugal to India, a British officer saw a man fall overboard. The crew threw the man a block of wood attached to a rope. As they were pulling him in, a shark attacked.

It killed the man. In his report, the officer described the attack.

After that 1580 attack, there were many other reports. One of the worst shark attacks in history was in 1945. The USS *Indianapolis* sailed in the Pacific Ocean during World War II (1939–1945). More than

The sinking of the USS Indianapolis led to one of the worst shark attacks in history.

Historians believe oceanic whitetip sharks attacked the survivors of the USS Indianapolis. *These sharks can be aggressive toward humans.*

1,000 sailors were aboard. The ship was hit by torpedoes and began to sink. Nearly 900 of the men jumped into the ocean. They were alone in the water for four days. Sharks attacked the swimming sailors. By the time rescue came, only 316 men survived.

One of the survivors was Loel Dean Cox. In an interview, he recalled what it was like to be surrounded by sharks. Cox said, "Every few minutes you'd see their fins—a dozen to two dozen fins in the water. They would come up and bump you. I was bumped a few times—you never know when they are going to attack you."[2]

WHY SHARKS ATTACK HUMANS

Sharks have great senses of hearing, smell, and touch. They can also see nearby objects well. They use these senses to explore their environment. They can detect both prey and other predators. Sharks also have another sense. It's called an **electrosensory system**. It works because all animals produce tiny amounts of electricity. A shark's electrosensory system can detect this electricity. If a prey animal twitches a muscle, the shark can sense it. This little twitch can make a hungry shark curious enough to check out what made it.

People once believed that sharks often attacked humans by accident. They thought sharks were mistaking humans for seals or sea lions. But scientists now believe a shark's senses would prevent these mistakes. Humans do not look like common shark prey. And they don't smell like prey animals either. But a shark may swim closer to a human to find out more. A quick bite would give it more information. Its taste buds will tell the shark whether this strange creature is worth eating.

THE MOVIE *JAWS* AND SHARK FEAR

In the summer of 1975, the movie *Jaws* came out. Moviegoers watched as a great white shark killed five people. This movie changed how people viewed sharks. Some were afraid to go in the water. They saw sharks as bloodthirsty hunters. Others decided to hunt sharks.

Shark experts have found no evidence that sharks hunt humans. But their research does suggest that there are at least two factors that increase the chance for an attack. One is increasing population. As the human population grows, more people are in the water. Gavin Naylor is the director of the Florida Program for Shark Research. He said, "The more sharks and people there are in one place, the greater the chance of them bumping into each other."[3]

The other major risk factor is the type of activity a person is doing. Some water activities are riskier than others.

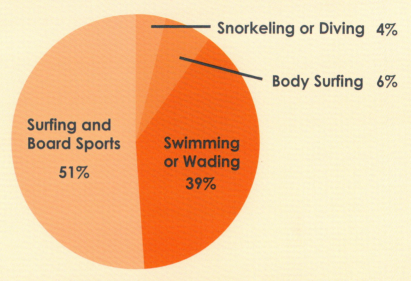

Source: "The ISAF 2021 Shark Attack Report," Florida Museum, January 24, 2022. www.floridamuseum.ufl.edu.

Some activities may put people more at risk of a shark attack than others. Surfers are often in areas that are commonly visited by sharks. Activities that involve a lot of splashing may also attract sharks.

The International Shark Attack File researches shark attacks. Its research found the risk was highest during surface activities. Surface activities include surfing and rafting. The next highest risk came

Many shark attacks happen near beaches. This is because there are many people in the water.

from swimming activities. These include swimming, wading, and playing in the water. The third highest risk came from diving activities.

There are two main types of shark attacks: provoked and unprovoked. In a provoked attack, the human bothers the shark. For example, a person tries to touch a shark. This causes the shark to attack. In an unprovoked attack, the shark attacks even though the human does nothing to bother it. Some researchers also list attacks that include watercraft, such as canoes, as a third type of attack.

WHERE, WHEN, AND HOW

Most shark attacks occur near the shore. That's where sharks tend to hunt. Attacks can also occur where the seafloor drops into deeper water. Sharks also find prey there. The United States is the country with

There are many movies, television shows, and books that describe shark attacks. One of the most famous is the movie Jaws.

the most shark attacks each year. Florida is the state with the most attacks. Sharks are more likely to attack at dawn and dusk. This is when they typically hunt.

There are three ways sharks generally attack. Hit-and-run attacks are the most common. They are also the least dangerous. The shark takes a bite and then swims away. The next two types are less common. They lead to greater injuries and more deaths. In a bump-and-bite attack, the shark circles, bumps into the victim, and then bites. In a sneak attack, the shark bites without warning. In these types of attacks, the shark often returns for more bites.

NOT SUCH A BIG RISK

News sources like to report on shark attacks. These stories are popular with readers. However, they can make it seem like shark attacks are a big threat. This can create a lot of fear. Worldwide, sharks kill an average of about ten people a year.

In contrast, other animals pose a much bigger threat. They hurt more people worldwide than sharks. For example, mosquitos can carry and spread diseases. They cause more than 700,000 deaths a year. Snakes kill at least 50,000 people. Dogs with the disease rabies kill about 25,000 people yearly. Crocodiles cause about 1,000 deaths a year. Compared to these animals, sharks are a small threat to humans.

However, humans are a huge threat to sharks. Around the world, people kill about 100 million sharks each year. Many are killed for their shark fins. The fins are used to make shark fin soup. This soup is popular in some countries. Many sharks are also killed in an attempt to make beaches safer.

SHARKS AND MUSIC

Researchers have found that music played in shark movies affects how viewers see sharks. The study had people watch a clip from a shark documentary. For some, the clip had scary music. For others, it had happy music or silence. The viewers who heard the scary music had a more negative view of sharks.

2
THE MOST DANGEROUS SHARKS

The Florida Museum keeps track of shark attacks on humans. It releases lists of these attacks. The list says how many attacks were from each type of shark. But reports like these aren't perfect. It can be hard to tell what shark attacked a person.

A shark attack victim may misidentify the type of shark.

Experts don't agree on how many shark species there are. This can make it hard to tell different sharks apart. Some scientists say there are about 400 species. Others say there are more than 500. However, only about a dozen are considered dangerous

Some sharks will leave humans alone if they are not bothered. However, many shark attacks are unprovoked.

to humans. The top three are great white, tiger, and bull sharks.

GREAT WHITE SHARKS

Great white sharks tend to stay in the areas near the coast. They spend most of their time in **temperate** waters. But they are also found in the cold open ocean. Unlike most sharks, they are **endothermic**. This helps them deal with the changes in water temperature.

Great whites are quite large. They can grow to be 20 feet (6 m) or longer. Their attacks have occurred in coastal places around the world. A great white will often use the bump-and-bite style of attack. It swims below prey, making it hard for the prey to see it. It will ram the prey and quickly bite. The Florida Museum reports that by 2021, great whites had been involved in about 350 attacks. Fifty-seven of those were fatal.

ANY SHARK CAN BE DANGEROUS

Just a few shark species are thought to be a danger to humans. However, shark experts agree: all sharks are predators and can be dangerous. If provoked, they may attack and cause harm. A shark may just be curious. But a large body with sharp teeth can be a deadly combination.

TIGER SHARKS

Tiger sharks are often found in coastal areas and near large island chains. They are also found in river mouths where they can find plenty of prey. They eat a wide range of food such as fish, squid, sea birds, and garbage. This wide range makes them dangerous. Many sharks will lose interest in humans after one bite. Tiger sharks tend to bite multiple times.

Like great whites, tiger sharks are also large. They can grow to 14 feet (4.3 m) long. Their skin has a pattern that makes them hard to see. This helps them sneak up on prey. They are usually slow swimmers. But when close to prey, they use bursts of great speed. Their sneak attacks work very well for them. Tiger sharks had attacked

DIVING WITH GREAT WHITE SHARKS

Michael Rutzen dives with great white sharks. In an interview, he explained that he follows shark safety rules. People must stand their ground and keep eye contact. They must not run away from it like prey. And they must not go towards it like a predator. He said, "And what we discovered, they're not mindless killers. They're actually very intelligent animals and curious animals."

Source: Quoted in "The Great White | Extended Interview with Mike Rutzen," 60 Minutes Australia, September 14, 2014. www.youtube.com.

Bull sharks have short, stubby snouts. They sometimes ram prey before biting.

138 times in total by 2021. Thirty-six attacks were fatal.

BULL SHARKS

Bull sharks are usually found in shallow water close to shore. But unlike most sharks, they also swim up rivers. They've even been seen hundreds of miles upstream from the ocean. This means bull sharks may be in places people don't expect. The average length for bull sharks is 7.5 feet (2.3 m). However, some can be 10 feet (3 m) or more. The females are a little larger than the males.

Bull sharks have poor vision. This is not a problem, since their strong sense of smell helps them find prey. They often hunt in muddy water. This gives them an advantage. Prey may not see the sharks, but the sharks can smell the prey. This makes the bump-and-bite way of hunting their preferred method. The Florida Museum reports that by 2021 bull sharks had attacked people about 120 times. Of those attacks, twenty-six were fatal.

OTHER DANGEROUS SHARKS

Five more sharks are also thought to be dangerous. But based on actual shark attack data, they are much less so.

Blacktip sharks tend to swim close to shore. Like the more dangerous tiger shark, they are also found near river mouths. These sharks grow to be about 8 feet (2.4 m) long. By 2021, there had been about forty attacks on humans in total, but none were fatal.

Sand tiger sharks are mostly not aggressive. They rarely attack people unless they are annoyed first.

Sand tiger sharks are mostly found in warm ocean waters. They are often found in shallow bays and near coral and rocky **reefs**. They grow to about 10 feet (3 m) long. Their teeth are sharp as razors and are great for cutting apart prey. There had been thirty-six attacks on humans in total by 2021. Like blackfin sharks, none of the attacks were fatal.

Blue sharks can grow to more than 13 feet (4 m) long. Blues pose a big threat to shipwrecks. As stranded humans float in the open ocean, these sharks are often the first on the scene. By 2021, blue sharks had attacked humans thirteen times. Four attacks were fatal.

Oceanic whitetips can be a threat to human divers. Divers have described being circled by the sharks. The circling sharks can be very hard to scare away. There had been fifteen attacks on humans by 2021. Three were fatal. Oceanic whitetips can be more than 12 feet (3.7 m) long.

Shortfin makos are named for their small dorsal fins.

Swimming up to 20 miles per hour (32 kmh), shortfin makos are one of the fastest sharks. Found in deep ocean waters, they can be up to 13 feet (4 m) long. Deep-sea fishers need to be careful. Once it's caught, a mako becomes violent in the water. It can harm the fisher. By 2021, shortfin makos had attacked nine humans. One attack was fatal.

3
LIVED TO TELL

Shark attacks occur all over the world. The International Shark Attack File keeps careful data on attacks that are reported worldwide. Its 2021 report showed the top eight countries for shark attacks. The United States had the most attacks with forty-seven. Australia ranked second with twelve attacks. Brazil, New Zealand, and South Africa each reported three. Canada, Ecuador, Saint Kitts and Nevis, and the French territory New Caledonia each reported one attack.

New Smyrna Beach in Florida has been called the "Shark Attack Capital of the World." Sharks are spotted in the water almost daily.

UNITED STATES

For decades, the United States has had the most shark attacks worldwide. In 2021, its forty-seven cases counted as more than half the world total. Of these attacks, only one was fatal. Florida alone had twenty-eight shark attacks. None were fatal.

3,000-YEAR-OLD SHARK ATTACK VICTIM

Scientists in Japan discovered a 3,000-year-old human skeleton in 2021. It had about 790 bite marks. The scientists determined the marks matched those often left by sharks. The skeleton was also missing a left hand and right leg. The scientists believe that a great white or tiger shark left the marks.

In May 2021, Adrienne Wikso was sitting on her paddleboard at a beach in Florida. A shark swam up, bit her foot, and pulled on it. Still on her board, Wikso kicked the shark with her free foot. A brave friend pushed her back to shore. It was a scary trip. Wikso said, "I was bleeding really bad and [the shark] was in the trail, the blood trail, and who knew if this guy was following us?"[4] She was taken to a hospital, where she had surgery on her foot.

Another Florida attack occurred three months later. Gretta Lowry was out on her surfboard. She was paddling back to shore

Sharks often hunt in the surf zone. This makes them a potential danger for surfers.

when a shark rammed into her board.

"The shark bit me twice, once on the thigh and then on the calf. It all happened so fast, I never even saw the shark and didn't have any time to react during the attack."[5]

Lowry was rushed to the hospital. Two months after the attack, Lowry returned to the water to surf.

Not all of America's shark attacks take place in Florida. In June 2021, Nemanja Spasojevic was snorkeling in California. As he was swimming, he felt a pain in his leg. Looking down, he saw the face of a great white shark. He kicked wildly and the shark swam away. At first, Spasojevic thought the bite was not serious. But when he got to shore, he saw his **wet suit** was filled with blood. A nearby fisherman called 911. At the hospital, doctors treated about ten deep cuts to his right thigh. His wounds healed, but he still walks with a limp.

AUSTRALIA

Australia had the second-most shark attacks worldwide in 2021. Six occurred in the state of New South Wales. Four were in Western Australia. The other two attacks happened in other states.

In January 2021, Cameron Wrathall was swimming in the Swan River in Western Australia. Without warning, a bull shark rammed and bit him. "The shark hit me really hard, it's the biggest impact I've ever

Shark bites often have a crescent shape.

felt of something hitting me," Wrathall said.[6] He had long and deep wounds. His hip was broken, and he couldn't move his leg. Doctors expected Wrathall to need two years of treatment to walk normally again.

Two months later, a second attack occurred in Western Australia. Gary May was on his paddleboard. A shark suddenly struck his board and gripped it in its mouth. May was thrown into the water and onto the shark's head. He jumped back on the board. The shark let go of the board. A surfer came by and helped him paddle back to shore. May was not hurt, but his board had large bite marks.

A third attack happed in Western Australia that June. Alex Dodds was spearfishing. He was diving when he saw a large shark below him. Before he could escape, the shark bit him below his left knee. Instead of biting again, the shark left. Dodds was flown to a hospital. He received one hundred stitches for his wound.

SHARK ATTACK RESPONSE INCORPORATED

Shark Attack Response Inc. is an organization in New South Wales, Australia. The group supplies first aid boxes to beaches. They can be used by **first responders** when there is a shark attack. The group is run by volunteers and depends on donations to keep it running.

4
STAYING SAFE IN THE WATER

The chance that a shark will attack someone is slim. Even so, people should be careful when in or near the water. Shark researchers have gathered the best advice for avoiding sharks.

BEFORE GETTING IN THE WATER

Shark safety begins before people even get into the water. Some places are more dangerous than others. For example, the mouths of rivers tend to be cloudy and full of fish and other prey. The cloudy water makes it hard to see sharks.

Very few people who visit beaches will ever experience shark attacks. Taking steps to be safe can lower the risk of a shark attack even more.

It's also a good idea to avoid activities near fishing boats. Fish often struggle when caught. Struggling fish attract sharks. Fishers will also toss fish they don't want into the water. This can attract sharks. Seabirds diving into the water can be another warning sign. The birds are diving for fish. If fish are there, sharks may also be around.

People should never swim, surf, or dive alone. Anyone who is injured will need someone to help them. People should also avoid being in the water at dawn or dusk. This is top feeding time for sharks.

Researchers believe bright colors like yellow or white make people more visible to sharks.

When going in the water, people should be mindful of what they wear. Bright swimsuits are fun but can attract sharks. Neon colors stand out in the water. Shiny jewelry can too. This is because jewelry reflects light. This makes it look like fish scales.

Many beaches close after an attack or a shark sighting. They may use signs to warn visitors of sharks.

WHEN IN THE WATER

It's important for people to pay attention while in the water. They should keep looking around and be ready to respond. If something doesn't seem right, they should get out immediately.

People in the water should watch for dolphins and porpoises. This can be an early warning sign for sharks. Dolphins and porpoises often feed on the same prey as sharks. If they are near, a shark may be hunting nearby.

While in the water, people should stay close to shore. That way if something goes wrong, it will be easier to get help. People who are bleeding or cut themselves should leave the water. Blood can attract sharks.

If someone is playing or swimming in the water, experts recommend avoiding splashing or moving quickly. A shark may think the splashing is from an animal in trouble. It will swim closer to investigate.

IF A SHARK COMES CLOSE OR ATTACKS

Even though a shark attack is unlikely, it's wise to be prepared. Experts recommend a few important actions if a shark comes close or attacks. First, people should not panic. They should avoid splashing. This could draw the shark closer. If the shark

SHARK CHASER

In the 1940s, the US Navy created a shark **repellent**. It was called Shark Chaser. Its chemicals smelled like a dead, rotting shark. Unfortunately, it didn't work. Still, the US military gave it out for about thirty years. As of 2021, there was no 100 percent effective shark repellent.

comes near, people should try to maintain eye contact. Sharks like to sneak up on prey. They may be less likely to attack if they know their targets can see them coming.

If a shark does attack, people should fight back. Paul de Gelder is a shark expert. He even advises punching the shark. "Anything that shows the shark you won't take it," he says. "Maybe you'll get out."[7]

SHARK ATTACK RESEARCH

There are many groups doing shark research worldwide. Some aim to reduce shark-human conflicts. To do this,

Some beaches have shark bite kits. This helps emergency crews treat victims more quickly.

researchers must first follow the sharks' movements. Often this is done through tags placed on the sharks.

These tags transmit shark movements to researchers. They show which sharks visited an area and when they came.

They also show how long they stayed at each place. Researchers then use that data to determine ways to reduce conflict. Sharing these strategies can help people and sharks enjoy the water safely.

Sharks can pose a danger to anyone who spends time in the ocean. However, only a few shark species have a record of attacks on humans. And of those attacks, few have led to deaths. People need to stay informed and follow the advice of shark experts. Such steps will reduce the risk of a shark attack.

GLOSSARY

electrosensory system

a system that can detect electricity

endothermic

able to maintain a constant body temperature independent of the environment

first responder

someone who is trained to respond to an emergency

reefs

areas of rock, coral, or sand near the surface of the ocean

repellent

a substance that makes an animal stay away

species

a group of animals of the same kind

temperate

having neither very hot nor very cold temperatures

wet suit

a tight-fitting suit made of rubber that is worn in cold water for warmth

SOURCE NOTES

INTRODUCTION: WHY STUDY SHARK ATTACKS?

1. Quoted in Julius Whigham II, "Shark-Bite Victim 'Happy to Be OK' After Incident Near Juno Beach Pier, Surgery on Arm," *Palm Beach Post*, March 19, 2021. www.palmbeachpost.com.

CHAPTER ONE: HOW BIG A RISK?

2. Quoted in Alex Last, "USS *Indianapolis* Sinking: 'You Could See Sharks Circling,'" *BBC News*, July 29, 2013. www.bbc.com.

3. Quoted in Richard Gray, "The Real Reasons Why Sharks Attack Humans," *BBC Future*, August 8, 2019. www.bbc.com.

CHAPTER THREE: LIVED TO TELL

4. Quoted in "Surfer Bitten by Bull Shark off Florida Beach," *CBS Miami*, May 5, 2021. https://miami.cbslocal.com.

5. Quoted in Airman 1st Class Thomas Sjoberg, "Police Officer Aids Shark Bite Victim at Florida Beach," *Space Launch Delta 45*, n.d. www.patrick.spaceforce.mil.

6. Quoted in "Swan River Shark Victim Cameron Wrathall 'Died' After Brutal Attack," *PerthNow*, February 8, 2021. www.perthnow.com.au.

CHAPTER FOUR: STAYING SAFE IN THE WATER

7. Quoted in Jake Rossen, "5 Expert Tips for Surviving a Shark Attack," *Mental Floss*, July 14, 2021. www.mentalfloss.com.

FOR FURTHER RESEARCH

BOOKS

Brian Skerry, *The Ultimate Book of Sharks*. Washington, DC: National Geographic, 2018.

Chelsea Xie, *Shark Biology*. San Diego, CA: BrightPoint Press, 2023.

Karen Romano Young, *Shark Quest: Protecting the Ocean's Top Predators*. Minneapolis, MN: Twenty-First Century Books, 2018.

INTERNET SOURCES

Richard Gray, "The Real Reasons Why Sharks Attack Humans," *BBC Future*, August 8, 2019. www.bbc.com/future.

Sabrina Imbler, "To Err Is Human; To Mistakenly Bite Is Baby White Shark," *New York Times*, October 27, 2021. www.nytimes.com.

"Why Are We So Afraid of Sharks?" *Nature Conservancy Australia*, n.d. www.natureaustralia.org.au.

WEBSITES

Atlantic White Shark Conservancy
www.atlanticwhiteshark.org

This group follows the activity of great white sharks. It uses its research to reduce shark-human conflict.

International Shark Attack File
www.floridamuseum.ufl.edu/shark-attacks

The International Shark Attack File covers a wide range of shark attack information. Topics include maps and data, shark attack trends, and how to report a shark attack.

Shark Stewards
https://sharkstewards.org

Shark Stewards work to protect sharks and their habitats. This site includes both information and ways to help.

INDEX

1580 attack, 12–13

Albert, Bryce, 6–9
Australia, 38, 44–47

blacktip shark, 9, 34
blood, 41, 43, 53
blue sharks, 36
bull sharks, 28, 32–34, 44
bump-and-bite attacks, 23, 29, 33

Cox, Loel Dean, 15

Dodds, Alex, 46–47
dolphins, 52–53

fatal attacks, 29, 32, 34–37, 40
fishing, 37, 43, 46, 50
Florida Museum, the, 19, 26, 29, 33

great white sharks, 17, 28–30, 31, 40, 43

hit-and-run attacks, 22
hunting, 17, 18, 21–22, 33, 53

Jaws, 17

Lowry, Gretta, 41–43

May, Gary, 46

oceanic whitetips, 36

prey, 16–17, 21, 29–31, 33, 35, 49, 53, 55

safety, 10, 25, 31, 49–57
sand tiger sharks, 35
senses
  electrosensory system, 16
  hearing, 15
  sight, 15, 33
  smell, 15, 17, 33
  touch, 15
shark tags, 56–57
shortfin makos, 37
sneak attacks, 23, 30–31, 55
Spasojevic, Nemanja, 43–44
speed, 31, 37

tiger sharks, 28, 30–32, 34, 40

United States, 21, 38, 40–44
USS *Indianapolis*, 13–15

water activities
  snorkeling, 19, 43
  surfing, 19, 41, 43, 46, 50
  swimming, 19–20, 43–44, 50, 53
Wikso, Adrienne, 41
Wrathall, Cameron, 44–45

IMAGE CREDITS

Cover: © Sergey Uryadnikov/Shutterstock Images
5: © Jim Agronick/Shutterstock Images
7: © Product Image Pro/iStockphoto
8: © Yann Hubert/Shutterstock Images
11: © Vision Dive/Shutterstock Images
13: National Archives/Naval History and Heritage Command/US Navy
14: © Martin Rejzek/Shutterstock Images
19: © Red Line Editorial
20: © Tupungato/Shutterstock Images
22: © Universal Pictures/Zanuck Brown Productions/Ronald Grant Archive/Alamy
27: © Fiona Ayerst/Shutterstock Images
32: © Fiona Ayerst/Shutterstock Images
35: © Stefan Pircher/Shutterstock Images
37: © Xavier Elias Photography/Shutterstock Images
39: © Sky Cinema/Shutterstock Images
42: © Trubavin/Shutterstock Images
45: © David Royal/Monterey County Herald/AP Images
49: © Fimina Anna/Shutterstock Images
51: © Javibruce/Shutterstock Images
52: © Spencer Weiner/AP Images
56: © MD Photography/Shutterstock Images

ABOUT THE AUTHOR

Gail Terp is the author of more than seventy nonfiction books for children. A retired elementary teacher, she now enjoys writing about all sorts of topics, such as people, science, history, and all things of the natural world. She also likes to search out fun and quirky books to recommend to her family and friends. When not reading and writing, she walks around looking for interesting stuff to write about.